Other Words

2nd edition

Leigh Tonks

Illustrated by Stephen Michael King

Thanks to Barb

Copyright © Leigh Tonks / Macmillan Science and Education Australia 2008
Macmillan Other Words 2nd edition
ISBN 978 1 4202 6501 9

Edited by Victoria Morgan
Design by Trish Hayes and Stephen Michael King
Illustrations by Stephen Michael King

Printed in Australia by Pegasus Media & Logistics
1 2 3 4 5 6 7 25 24

CONTENTS

INTRODUCTION

How can *Other Words* help you?

⭐ It can help you to find great words to use when you are writing.

⭐ It can help you to stop using the same words too often; for example, words such as *big, nice* and *said*.

⭐ It can help you to write what you are really thinking and feeling.

....

What is in this book?

1. OTHER WORDS

These are lists of words that are similar in meaning to the one that you are looking up. Read through the lists until you find the best word to use.

2. APPENDIXES

The appendixes feature useful wordlists that show different types of particular things. For example, if you look up **dogs** you will find different types of dogs you can have — from an Afghan through to a wolfhound!

3. INDEX

The index in the back of the book features a list of words that writers often use when they are writing. All of these words are good to use sometimes, but they can usually be replaced by words that are more precise or interesting. The index helps you find these words.

OTHER WORDS

accident
noun

avalanche
calamity
catastrophe
clash
collision
crash
disaster
explosion
fall
fatality
misfortune
mishap
pile-up
smash
tragedy

angry
adjective

annoyed
bitter
cross
discontented
disgruntled
displeased
enraged
fed up
fierce
fiery
fuming
furious
incensed
indignant
infuriated
irate
irritated
livid
mad
raging
ropeable
savage
spiteful

animal
noun

amphibian
beast
carnivore
creature
game
herbivore
insect
invertebrate
mammal
marsupial
pest
pet
primate
reptile
rodent
vermin
vertebrate

Hint! *For specific types of animals see the Appendix.*

argue
verb

answer back
antagonise
bicker
clash
conflict
confront
contradict
debate
differ
disagree
dispute
gang up on
go on strike
have words
object to
protest
quarrel
quibble
row

attach
verb

adhere
bind
bond
brace
fasten
seal
secure
settle
solder
steady
stick

attack
verb

advance on
ambush
assault
battle
beat up
besiege
charge
declare war
fly at
gang up on
hit
invade
mug
pick on
pillage
plunder
raid
riot
run at
savage
set on
storm
swoop on
threaten
turn on

attractive
adjective

alluring
beautiful
cute
elegant
exquisite
glamorous
good-looking
gorgeous
handsome
heavenly
inviting
lovely
pretty
stunning

bad
adjective

abusive
appalling
atrocious
awful
chronic
corrupt
criminal
cruel
decayed
defective
deplorable
despicable
detestable
diabolic
disastrous
disgraceful
disgusting
dishonest
dreadful
evil
faulty
foul
fiendish
harmful
hopeless
horrible
illegal
immoral
imperfect
inexcusable

lousy
mean
mischievous
nasty
naughty
pathetic
poisonous
poor
putrid
repulsive
revolting
rotten
severe
shameful
shocking
sick
sinister
terrible
unacceptable
unfair
unforgivable
unsatisfactory
useless
vile
wicked
wretched

Hint! *You can form adverbs by adding* **–ly** *or* **–ily** *to many of the adjectives on this page.*

bend
noun

angle
arc
arch
bow
buckle
corner
curve
distortion
dogleg
fold
fork
hairpin bend
kink
loop
turn
wave

bend
verb

arch
bow
buckle
contort
curl
curve
distort
flex
hook

loop
misshape
move
rotate
screw
spin
swing
turn
twist
warp
wind

big
adjective

broad
bulky
chubby
colossal
enormous
expansive
extensive
fat
giant
gigantic
great
gross
heavy
high
huge
immense
important

jumbo
king-size
large
long
mammoth
massive
mighty
monstrous
monumental
obese
substantial
swollen
tall
thick
towering
vast
wide

bicycle
noun

BMX bike
cycle
dragster
mountain bike
penny-farthing
pushbike
racer
tandem
three-wheeler
tricycle
trike
unicycle

bit
noun

atom
chip
crumb
dab
dash
dot
dribble
drop
fleck
fraction
fragment
grain
molecule
morsel

mouthful
part
particle
patch
peck
percentage
piece
pinch
portion
proportion
ration
scrap
share
sliver
snippet
spark
speck
trace

blow
verb

blast
breathe
exhale
gasp
heave
hiss
pant
puff
respire
sigh
whistle

boring
adjective

barren
bland
common
drab
dreary
dull
featureless
lifeless
monotonous
plain
repetitious
tedious
uninspiring
uninteresting

bottom
noun

base
basis
basement
bedrock
downstairs
floor
foot
foundation
minimum
seabed
sea floor
underside
undercarriage

brave
adjective

adventurous
audacious
bold
courageous
daring
fearless
gallant
game
heroic
intrepid
lion-hearted
plucky
undaunted
valiant

break
verb

batter
burst
crack
crash
crush
cut
destroy
disassemble
disconnect
disintegrate
disrupt
divide
explode
force

fracture
grind
mash
pound
pulverise
ruin
rupture
separate
sever
shatter
smash
snap
splinter
split up
tear
wreck
wrench

bright
adjective

brilliant
colourful
dazzling
fiery
flaming
fluorescent
gaudy
glary
glassy
gleaming
glossy
glowing
illuminated
iridescent
light
luminous
psychedelic
radiant
shining
shiny
silvery
sparkling
vivid

broken
adjective

cracked
crushed
damaged
dilapidated
defective
faulty
fractured
fragmented
impaired
out of order
ruined
ruptured
shattered
snapped
split
torn
wrecked

burn
verb

blaze
char
cremate
flare
glow
ignite
incinerate
kindle
roast
scald
scorch
singe
sizzle
smoke
smoulder
toast

Hint! *To see the adjective **bright** used in another way see **clever**, page 15.*

calm
adjective

balanced
composed
controlled
cool
easygoing
gentle
harmonious
level-headed
mild
motionless
peaceful
placid
quiet
relaxed
sedate
self-composed
serene
stable
steady
still
tranquil
unfussed
unruffled

catch
verb

ambush
apprehend
arrest
capture
grab
grip
kidnap
pounce on
seize
snag
snare
take prisoner
trap

change
verb

adapt
adjust
affect
alter
amend

convert
correct
edit
exchange
manipulate
modify
mutate
rectify
reform
revise
revolutionise
shift
substitute
swap
switch
transfer
transform
transplant
turn
twist
vary

cheap
adjective

affordable
cut-price
discounted
inexpensive
marked down
reduced

cheat
verb

bluff
con
deceive
defraud
delude
doublecross
embezzle
fool
hoodwink
mislead
rip off
swindle
tamper
trick

clean
adjective

clear
fresh
hygienic
immaculate
impeccable
pure
refined
sanitary
spotless
stainless
sterile
sterilised
unblemished
uncontaminated
unpolluted
unsoiled
unspoilt

clean
verb

buff
brush
degrease
disinfect
distil
dry-clean
dust
filter
flush
mop
polish
purify
rinse
sanitise
scour
scrub
shampoo
sponge
spring-clean
sterilise
sweep
vacuum
wash
wipe

14

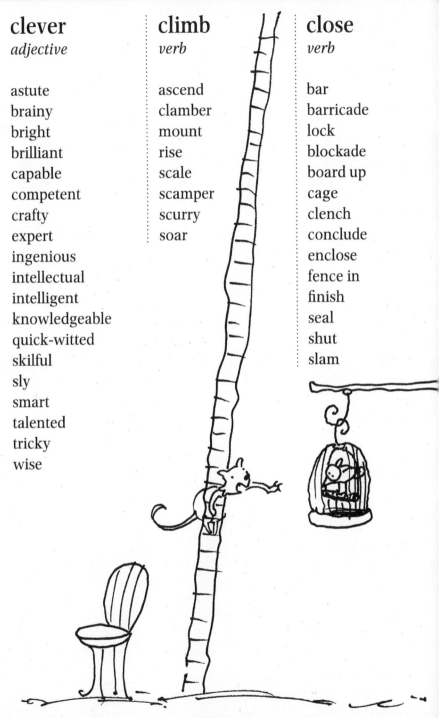

clever
adjective

astute
brainy
bright
brilliant
capable
competent
crafty
expert
ingenious
intellectual
intelligent
knowledgeable
quick-witted
skilful
sly
smart
talented
tricky
wise

climb
verb

ascend
clamber
mount
rise
scale
scamper
scurry
soar

close
verb

bar
barricade
lock
blockade
board up
cage
clench
conclude
enclose
fence in
finish
seal
shut
slam

coastline
noun

bay
beach
bight
cape
coral reef
cove
estuary
gulf
foreshore
headland
inlet
peninsula
promontory
reef
sand dunes
seashore
seaside
shore
waterfront

cold
adjective

bleak
chilled
chilly
cool
freezing

fresh
frigid
frostbitten
frosty
frozen
glacial
ice-cold
icy
nippy
snowy
wintry

come
verb

appear
approach
arrive
berth
disembark
emerge
land
move
reach
touchdown
turn up
visit

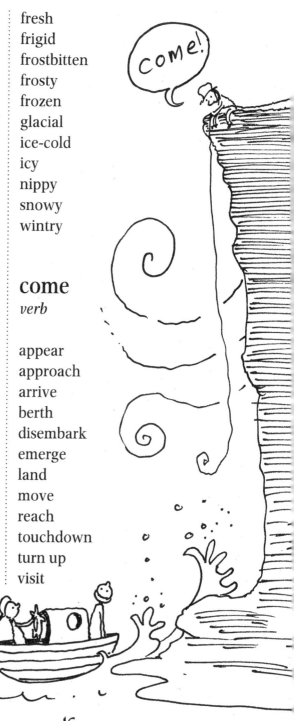

come!

commotion
noun

anarchy
bedlam
chaos
confusion
disorder
disturbance
fracas
fuss
mix-up
muddle
pandemonium
ruckus
tangle
tempest
turmoil

container
noun

backpack
bag
barrel
basin
bin
bottle
bowl
box
bucket
cabinet
cage
can
carton
case
casket
cauldron
chest
coffin
crate
cupboard
dish
drum

enclosure
flask
hamper
holster
jar
jug
keg
kettle
letterbox
locker
matchbox
medicine chest
moneybox
pot
sack
saddlebag
saucepan
scabbard
tank
trunk
trough
tub
urn
vase
vat
vessel

cook
verb

bake
barbecue
boil
braise
brew
broil
brown
burn
deep-fry
fry
grill
hard-boil
heat up
microwave
overheat
pan-fry
poach
prepare
roast
sauté
scramble
sear
simmer
steam
stew
stir-fry
toast

copy
verb

ape
counterfeit
duplicate
imitate
impersonate
match
mimic
mirror
photocopy
replicate
reproduce
simulate
trace
transcribe

criminal
noun

accessory
bandit
burglar
bushranger
convict
culprit
delinquent
felon
fiend
gangster
graffiti artist
highwayman
hooligan
inmate
killer
mobster
murderer
offender
outlaw
pickpocket
prisoner
robber
rogue
scoundrel
shoplifter
thief
thug
trespasser
vandal
villain

crooked
adjective

angled
askew
bent
bowed
buckled
coiled
curled
curved
distorted
hooked
kinked
looped
misshapen
twisted
warped
wavy
winding

cry
verb

bawl
bellow
blubber
call
grieve
howl
lament
moan
mope
roar
sob
scream
screech
shriek
snivel
sniffle
wail
weep
whimper
whine

cut
noun

break
chip
crack
crevice
fissure
fracture
gap
hole
incision
laceration
nick
notch
opening
perforation
rip
slash
slice
slit
tear
wound

cut
verb

axe
behead
carve
chip
chisel
chop
claw
clip
decapitate
dice
divide
fell
gash
gouge
graze
hack
knife
lacerate
lance
log
mow
mutilate
nick
prune
rip
saw
score
scratch
sever
shave

shear
slash
slice
slit
snick
snip
stab
tear
trim
whittle
wound

> **Hint!** *To see the verb* **cut** *used in another way see* **decrease**, *page 21.*

dangerous
adjective

contaminated
critical
deadly
desperate
fatal
harmful
hazardous
lethal
malignant
noxious
ominous
perilous
poisonous

precarious
toxic
risky
serious
threatening
unsafe
venomous

dark
adjective

black
blackened
burnt
brunette
cloudy
dim
dismal
dull
ebony
inky
jet black
murky
opaque
overcast
pitch-black
shaded
shadowy
shady
sombre
sooty
starless

dead
adjective

at peace
at rest
deceased
departed
extinct
fallen
inanimate
late
lifeless

decide
verb

choose
conclude
determine
elect
opt for
pick
prefer
resolve
select
settle
take

decrease
verb

cut
cut back
deduct
discount
lessen
lower
reduce
minimise
prune
scale down
subtract
taper
whittle

delicious
adjective

appetising
delightful
enjoyable
flavoursome
luscious
mouth-watering
savoury
scrumptious
spicy
sweet
tasty
yummy

die
verb

choke
drown
expire
pass away
perish
starve
suffocate
wither

difficult
adjective

advanced
adverse
arduous
backbreaking
challenging
complex
complicated
confusing
demanding
diabolic
formidable
grievous
hard
harsh
laborious
perplexing
rugged
severe
tough
troublesome
trying

dig
verb

burrow
cut
delve
dredge
excavate
fossick
gouge
hoe
mine
plough
quarry
scoop
shovel
tunnel
unearth

dirty
adjective

black
contaminated
dingy
dusty
filthy
foul
greasy
grimy
grotty
grubby
impure
infected
messy
muddy
murky
offensive
polluted
putrid
rotting
slimy
smeared
smoky
smudged
soiled
stagnant
unclean
unsanitary
untidy
unwashed

drink
verb

consume
devour
gulp
guzzle
lap
sip
slurp
suck
swallow
swig
taste
toast

dry
adjective

arid
barren
bone-dry
dehydrated
parched
sunbaked
thirsty
waterless
withered

easy
adjective

effortless
foolproof
manageable
simple
uncomplicated
undemanding

eat
verb

bite
chew
consume
devour
dine
gobble
gorge
graze
gulp
masticate
munch
nibble
overeat
swallow
taste
wolf

edge
noun

bank
border
boundary
brim
brink
circumference
coast
extremity
flank
fringe
frontier
horizon
kerb
ledge
limit
lip
margin
outline
outside
outskirts
perimeter
periphery
rim
seashore
shore
side
sideline
verge

23

empty
adjective

blank
clear
deserted
exhausted
finished
hollow
uninhabited
unoccupied
used up
vacant
void

enemy
noun

antagonist
archenemy
attacker
adversary
foe
opponent
rebel
rival
terrorist
traitor
troublemaker

exciting
adjective

awe-inspiring
breathtaking
exhilarating
mind-blowing
nail-biting
sensational
stimulating
stirring
startling
thrilling
vibrant

excited
adjective

agitated
exhilarated
fluttery
frenzied
hectic
hyperactive
jittery
jumpy
overwrought
restless
stimulated
thrilled
worked up

expert
noun

ace
authority
consultant
genius
hot shot
maestro
prodigy
professional
scientist
specialist
technician
veteran
virtuoso
whiz-kid

fall
noun

collapse
crash
decline
defeat
descent
dip
dive
drop
lapse
nosedive
sag
slip
slump
stumble
trip
tumble

fall
verb

capsize
cave in
collapse
crash-land
descend
drop
flop
free-fall
overbalance
parachute
sink
slip
slump
stumble
subside
topple
trip
tumble

fair
adjective

authentic
correct
decent
democratic
diplomatic
even
equal
genuine
honest
impartial
honourable
just
justifiable
lawful
legitimate
moral
neutral
objective
proper
reasonable
right
satisfactory
sincere
sporting
unbiased

fast
adjective

brisk
express
fleet
hasty
high-speed
jet-propelled
meteoric
prompt
quick
rapid
speedy
sudden
swift

fat
adjective

fleshy
heavy
obese
plump
portly
rotund
stout
thickset
tubby
well-built

fence
noun

barbed wire fence
barricade
barrier
blockade
boundary
cyclone fence
electric fence
gate
guardrail
hurdle
obstacle
picket fence
roadblock
shark net
wall

fight
noun

argument
attack
battle
bout
brawl
campaign
clash
combat
conflict
contest
controversy
debate
disagreement
dispute
duel
feud
gunfight
incident
invasion
massacre
misunderstanding
quarrel
raid
row
ruckus
scuffle
shoot-out
skirmish
squabble
struggle

tussle
war
wrangle

fight
verb

argue
attack
battle
bicker
box
brawl
combat
conflict
contest
defend
differ
dispute
duel
feud
go to war
grapple
make a stand
punch
quarrel
retaliate
scuffle
spar
struggle
tussle
wrangle
wrestle

find
verb

ascertain
compute
conclude
deduce
detect
discover
expose
extract
figure out
learn
locate
realise
recognise
resolve
see
solve
spot
trace
track down
unearth

fix
verb

amend
arrange
correct
improve
mend
patch
rectify
reform
remedy
renew
renovate
repair
restore
service
sew
upgrade

Hint! *To see the verb* **fix** *used in another way see* **attach**, *page 6.*

27

flow
verb

bleed
course
drain
dribble
drip
flood
gush
haemorrhage
jet
lap
ooze
overflow
pour
run
seep
spill
splash
spout
spurt
squirt
stream
swirl
trickle
wash

fly
verb

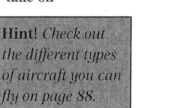

ascend
descend
dive
flap
flit
flutter
glide
hang-glide
hover
land
lift off
soar
swarm
take off

Hint! *Check out the different types of aircraft you can fly on page 88.*

follow
verb

chase
haunt
hunt
pursue
search
seek
shadow
trace
track
trail

food
noun

afternoon tea
banquet
breakfast
coffee break
delicacy
diet
dinner
fast food
feast
finger food
health food
junk food
lunch
meal
midnight feast
morning tea
nourishment
nutrition
picnic
play lunch
provisions
rations
recess
refreshment
smorgasbord
snack
supper
tea

friend
noun

acquaintance
ally
associate
boyfriend
collaborator
colleague
companion
comrade
girlfriend
mate
neighbour
pal
partner
penfriend
playmate
sweetheart

full
adjective

ample
brimming
bulging
bursting
crammed
crowded
full up
generous
jam-packed
laden
loaded
occupied
overflowing
packed
topped up

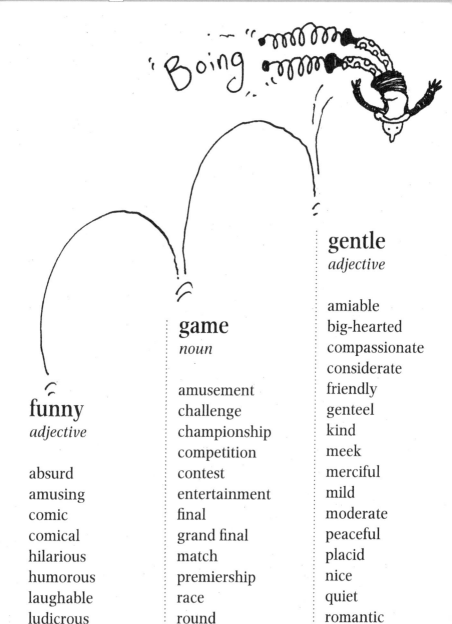

"Boing"

gentle
adjective

amiable
big-hearted
compassionate
considerate
friendly
genteel
kind
meek
merciful
mild
moderate
peaceful
placid
nice
quiet
romantic
slight
sweet
tender
thoughtful

game
noun

amusement
challenge
championship
competition
contest
entertainment
final
grand final
match
premiership
race
round
recreation
sport
test match
tournament

funny
adjective

absurd
amusing
comic
comical
hilarious
humorous
laughable
ludicrous
side-splitting
slapstick
uproarious
witty

get
verb

accept
achieve
acquire
attain
borrow
bring
buy
capture
catch
collect
confiscate
earn
fetch
find
gain
gather
grab
harvest
inherit
obtain
pick
pinch
pocket
possess
purchase
receive
recover
secure
seize
snatch
steal
take
win

give
verb

allocate
allow
assign
award
bestow
contribute
convey
deliver
dispense
distribute
divide
donate
grant
issue
offer
present
provide
ration
sacrifice
serve out
share

good
adjective

bright
clever
considerate
decent
dependable
devoted
excellent
helpful
honest
honourable
humane
kind
loyal
nice
pure
reliable
right
smart
thoughtful
virtuous

great
adjective

amazing
astonishing
astounding
divine
excellent
exceptional
exquisite
extraordinary
fabulous
fantastic
faultless
first-class
good
grand
ideal
immaculate
impeccable
important
incredible
magnificent
marvellous
mighty
miraculous
outstanding
overwhelming
perfect
phenomenal
prime
remarkable
sensational
splendid

startling
superb
superior
supreme
terrific
tremendous
unbelievable
wonderful

Hint! *To see the adjective **great** used in another way see **big**, page 8.*

To see the adjective **great** used in another way see **big**, page 8.

group
noun

assembly
association
assortment
audience
band
batch
battalion
body
branch
brigade
bunch
bundle
category
club
cluster
colony
committee

community
company
congregation
corps
corporation
crew
crowd
division
family
force
gang
gathering
heap
huddle
mass
mob
multitude
organisation
outfit
pack
parade
party
pile
platoon
regiment
set
society
squad
squadron
stack
throng
tribe
troop
union

grow
verb

accumulate
amplify
bloom
cultivate
develop
dilate
enlarge
escalate
expand
extend
improve
increase
multiply
mushroom
plant
progress
regenerate
reproduce
rise
spread
swell

happy
adjective

blissful
buoyant
carefree
cheerful
contented
delighted
ecstatic
elated
enchanted
glad
gleeful
jolly
jovial
joyful
joyous
merry
overjoyed
pleased
satisfied
thrilled

hard
adjective

compacted
firm
hardened
rigid
rocky
solid
starched
stiff
taut

Hint! *To see the adjective* **hard** *used in another way see* **difficult**, *page 22.*

hate
verb

abhor
despise
detest
dislike
loathe
object to

heavy
adjective

bulky
cumbersome
gross
hefty
laden
loaded
massive
overloaded
overweight
stocky
solid
weighty

help
noun

aid
assistance
backing
boost
charity
comfort
encouragement
favour
hand
protection
relief
service
sponsorship
support

help
verb

aid
assist
attend
back up
benefit
boost
care for
collaborate
comfort
cooperate
defend
encourage
improve
nurse
nurture
promote
provide for
reform
relieve
sponsor
support

helper
noun

adviser
aide
ally
assistant

associate
attendant
benefactor
companion
counsellor
deputy
farmhand
flight attendant
friend
housekeeper
jackaroo
jillaroo
maid
nurse
patron
porter
receptionist
secretary
servant
social worker
station hand
supporter
valet
waiter

34

hidden
adjective

blanketed
buried
camouflaged
censored
classified
concealed
confidential
covered
disguised
enveloped
hushed up
masked
obscured
out of sight
secluded
secret
stowed away
submerged
undercover
underground

hide
verb

blanket
burrow
bury
camouflage
conceal
cover up
disguise
enclose
envelop
hush up
keep a secret
lie low
lock up
mask
masquerade
obscure
screen
seclude
secrete
shade

hill
noun

bluff
cliff
crag
dune
headland
heap
highland
hilltop
incline
knoll
mound
mount
mountain
outcrop
peak
pinnacle
plateau
range
sand dune
tableland
volcano

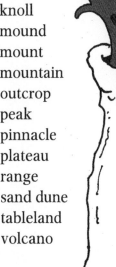

hit
verb

attack
bang
bash
bat
beat
belt
box
bump
cane
clip
clout
cuff
flog
hammer
knock
lash
pound
punch
ram
slam
slap
smack
smash
spank
strike
swat

thrash
thud
thump
wallop
whack
whip

hold
verb

arrest
clasp
clench
cling to
clutch
confine
contain
cuddle
detain
embrace
enclose
grab
grasp
grip
handle
hug
immobilise
imprison
keep
restrain
retain
seize
snatch

hole
noun

ant hole
blowhole
bore
burrow
cave
cavern
cavity
crack
crater
dugout
excavation
foxhole
gap
hollow
manhole
mine
trench
oilwell
opening
peephole
perforation
pinprick
pit
pothole
puncture
quarry
rabbit hole
shaft
tunnel
waterhole
well

horrible
adjective

appalling
awful
bad
beastly
bitter
bloodcurdling
creepy
distressing
dreadful
eerie
foul
frightening
frightful
ghastly
grim
grisly
gruesome
heartbreaking
horrendous
horrid
horrific
horrifying
intolerable
mean
monstrous
nasty
naughty
obnoxious
offensive
rank

repulsive
revolting
scary
shocking
sickening
smelly
spinechilling
spooky
terrible
terrifying
traumatic
unbearable
vile
wicked

hot
adjective

baking
blazing
blistering
burning
fiery
humid
muggy
oppressive
overheated
roasting
scalding
scorching
sultry
stifling
sweltering

hurry
verb

accelerate
bolt
chase
dart
dash
dive
fly
hasten
hurtle
race
run
rush
quicken
scamper
scoot
scramble
scurry
speed
sprint
streak
tear
urge
whip
whirl
zip
zoom

Hint! *You can form adverbs by adding –ly or –ily to many of the adjectives on this page.*

37

hurt
verb

ache
beat-up
bite
bruise
cripple
damage
distress
harm
impair
injure
lacerate
maim
mangle
mutilate
offend
pinch
prick
shatter
sprain
stab
sting
strain
tear
torture
traumatise
wound
wrench

important
adjective

big
considerable
critical
distinguished
eminent
famous
grand
great
grave
honourable
illustrious
impressive
main
memorable
momentous
newsworthy
notable
prestigious
prominent
reputable
respectable
serious
significant
special
unforgettable
valued

inhabit
verb

board
colonise
dwell
endure
exist
live in
lodge
occupy
populate
rent
reside
settle

38

injury
noun

agony
bite
black eye
blemish
bruise
burn
contusion
cut
disability
discomfort
dislocation
flesh wound
fracture
graze
handicap
harm
maiming
mutilation
pain
scratch
sprain
stab
strain
tear
trauma
welt
wound

inside
noun

centre
contents
core
entrails
guts
heart
hub
innards
innermost
interior
internal
intestines
kernel
middle
nucleus
soul

interesting
adjective

absorbing
appealing
attractive
bewitching
captivating
charismatic
charming
desirable
enchanting

engrossing
enthralling
enticing
eye-catching
fascinating
gripping
impressive
intriguing
inviting
irresistible
magnetic
mesmerising
remarkable
stimulating
tempting

jail
noun

cell
compound
concentration
 camp
dungeon
hulk
lockup
penal settlement
penitentiary
prison
prison farm

Hint! *Jail* *used*
to be spelt **gaol**.

job
noun

appointment
assignment
business
career
challenge
chore
craft
duty
employment
enterprise
errand
function
mission
obligation
occupation
operation
post
position
profession
project
responsibility
role
task
trade
vocation
work

join
verb

amalgamate
attach
blend
bridge
combine
connect
converge
fasten
fuse
glue
hinge
knit
link
match
mesh
mix
partner
paste
sew
stick
tie
unite
volunteer
weld

jump
verb

abseil
bob

bounce
bound
caper
drop
gambol
hop
hurdle
leap
leapfrog
parachute
pounce
prance
skip
trampoline
tumble
vault

keen
adjective

ambitious
anxious
ardent
avid
eager
enthusiastic
fanatical
passionate
raring
willing
zealous

BOING

keep
verb

bottle
confine
conserve
detain
guard
have
hold
imprison
maintain
preserve
refrigerate
retain
save
secure
store
withhold

kill
verb

assassinate
behead
butcher
choke
drown
electrocute
execute
exterminate
guillotine
hang
harpoon
knife
lynch
massacre
murder
poison
put down
shoot
slaughter
slay
smother
strangle
suffocate

lake
noun

billabong
bog
dam
lagoon
loch
marsh
pond
pool
quagmire
reservoir
swamp
waterhole

Hint! *The sea and ocean are much larger bodies of water.*

41

land
verb

alight
arrive
beach
berth
crash
descend
disembark
dismount
perch
reach
set down
settle
touchdown

laugh
verb

cackle
chortle
chuckle

fall about
giggle
grin
guffaw
howl
roar
shriek
smirk
sneer
snicker
snigger
titter

leader
noun

admiral
boss
captain
chairperson
chief
chieftain
colonel

commander
dictator
director
employer
emperor
empress
governor
inspector
judge
king
majesty
manager
mayor
minister
prefect
premier
president
prime minister
principal
queen
ruler
skipper
superior
supervisor

leave
verb

abandon
depart
desert
disappear
embark
emigrate
escape
evacuate
exit
flee
go
migrate
quit
resign
retire
retreat
set sail
vacate
withdraw

let
verb

allow
authorise
consent
license
permit
sanction
tolerate

lift
verb

boost
elevate
heave
heighten
hoist
lever
pick up
pull
raise
winch

light
noun

blaze
candlelight
daylight
firelight
flare
flash
flicker
gleam
glimmer
glint
glitter
glow
illumination
lustre
moonlight
radiance
shimmer
spark
sparkle
sunlight
sunshine
torchlight

like
verb

admire
adore
appreciate
care for
cherish
crave
desire
enjoy
fancy
long for
love
respect
treasure
welcome

little
adjective

baby
brief
compact
diminutive
dwarfish
insignificant
meagre
microscopic
mini
miniature
minor

minute
puny
short
skimpy
slight
small
stunted
thin
tiny
trivial
undersized

look at
verb

analyse
assess
behold
check
examine
explore
gaze
glance
glare
glimpse
inspect
investigate
notice
observe
ogle
peek
peep
recognise

review
scan
see
skim
spot
spy
squint
study
survey
stare
view
watch
witness

loud
adjective

audible
blaring
boisterous
deafening
forte
fortissimo
howling
loudmouthed
noisy
piercing
powerful
roaring
shrill
strong
thunderous
tumultuous

mad
adjective

agitated
angry
crazy
daft
delirious
demented
deranged
fanatical
foolhardy
frantic
frenzied
hot-headed
hysterical
insane
irate
irrational
lunatic
maniacal
nutty
odd
passionate
peculiar
psychotic
queer
rabid
raging
silly
wild

> **Hint!** *You can form adverbs by adding –ly or –ily to many of the adjectives on this page.*

make
verb

assemble
build
compose
conceive
construct
cook
create
design
develop
devise
do
erect
establish
fabricate
fashion
formulate
improvise
innovate
invent
manufacture
mould
originate
prepare
produce
shape
synthesise

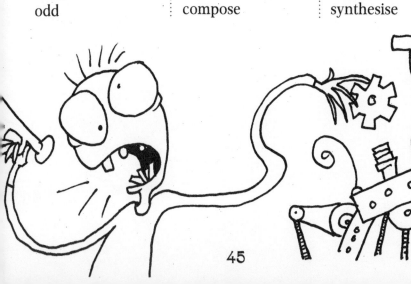

man
noun

adult
boyfriend
brother
buddy
chap
father
fellow
gentleman
grandfather
grandson
guy
husband
lad
male
master
mate
mister
nephew
person
son
uncle
youth

many
adjective

abounding
abundant
ample

bulk
considerable
copious
countless
endless
infinite
innumerable
lots
multiple
myriad
numerous
plentiful
plenty
profuse
prolific
uncounted
various

mean
adjective

bad
barbaric
beastly
brutal
callous
cold-blooded
cruel
cutthroat
despicable
ferocious
fiendish
fierce

hard
harsh
heartless
horrible
inhuman
malicious
merciless
nasty
naughty
pitiless
ruthless
sadistic
savage
selfish
severe
spiteful
stingy
unfeeling
vicious

Hint! *You will find words that are the opposite of* **mean** *on page 50 under* **nice**.

46

meet
verb

assemble
confront
congregate
connect
contact
converge
encounter
gather
group
join
unite

mess
noun

clutter
dirtiness
dump
filth
garbage
grime
jumble
litter
shambles
sprawl
squalor
untidiness

messy
adjective

bedraggled
chaotic
cluttered
dirty
dishevelled
disorderly
disorganised
filthy
jumbled
ragged
scattered
sloppy
untidy

mistake
noun

blunder
bungle
error
fault
inaccuracy
miscalculation
misconception
misunderstanding
oversight
slip

money
noun

banknote
bankroll
capital
cash
cents
change
cheque
coins
currency
dollars
expenses
finance
fortune
gold
income
loot
notes
petty cash
profit
revenue
riches
salary
savings
silver
small change
treasure

Hint! *To see the noun **mess** used in another way see **commotion**, page 17.*

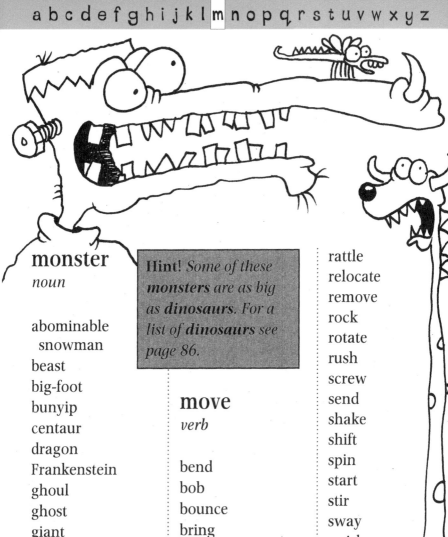

monster
noun

abominable
  snowman
beast
big-foot
bunyip
centaur
dragon
Frankenstein
ghoul
ghost
giant
Loch Ness monster
monstrosity
ogre
phantom
vampire
werewolf
yeti
yowie
zombie

Hint! *Some of these* **monsters** *are as big as* **dinosaurs**. *For a list of* **dinosaurs** *see page 86.*

move
verb

bend
bob
bounce
bring
budge
carry
collect
convey
go
jerk
jiggle
lift
lurch

rattle
relocate
remove
rock
rotate
rush
screw
send
shake
shift
spin
start
stir
sway
swirl
take
transfer
transport
turn
twirl
twist
walk
whip
wobble

naughty
adjective

abusive
bad
badly-behaved
cheeky
coarse
crude
delinquent
destructive
discourteous
disobedient
evil
horrible
ill-mannered
immoral
impertinent
impolite
improper
impudent
incorrigible
indecent
insolent
insulting
irresponsible
loutish
mean
mischievous
obscene
offensive
rebellious
rough
rude
sly
unacceptable
uncontrollable
uncooperative
undisciplined
vulgar
wicked

new
adjective

additional
another
bonus
brand-new
contemporary
current
fashionable
first
fresh
innovative
latest
modern
newly-formed
novel
original
raw
recent
state-of-the-art
trendy
unworn
up-to-date
young

> **Hint!** *You can form adverbs by adding –ly or –ily to many of the adjectives on this page.*

nice
adjective

adorable
attractive
charming
cheerful
compassionate
considerate
courteous
cultured
cute
decent
delightful
desirable
enjoyable
exquisite
friendly
generous
gentle
good-natured
heavenly
helpful
kind
likeable
lovely
modest
neighbourly
peaceful
picturesque
pleasing
polite
proper

refined
serene
sociable
sweet
tender
thoughtful
unselfish

noise
noun

bedlam
commotion
din
fuss
hubbub
hullabaloo
melee
outcry
pandemonium
racket
riot
row
ruckus
sound
tone
tune
turmoil
uproar

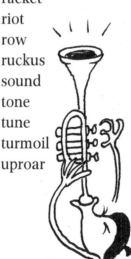

noises
noun

babble
bang
beep
blare
blast
boom
clang
clap
clash
crash
gurgle
hiss
howl
hum
laugh
moan
murmur
patter
rattle
roar
rumble
rustle
scream
screech
shriek
sigh
slurp
snore
snort
squeak

50

squeal
tinkle
twang
whisper
yap
yell

normal
adjective

accepted
all right
average
common
conventional
customary
everyday
mediocre
medium
mild
moderate
mundane
natural
ordinary
plain
standard
typical
usual

old
adjective

aged
ancient
antiquated
antique
archaic
classic
crumbling
dated
decayed
elderly
extinct
former
obsolete
old-fashioned
old-time
original
outdated
prehistoric
primitive
second-hand
stale
threadbare
veteran
vintage
weather-beaten
worn

open
verb

unbolt
unbutton
uncork
undo
unhook
unlock
unplug
unwrap
unzip

Gurgle
gurgle

Hint! *You can form adverbs by adding* **–ly** *or* **–ily** *to many of the adjectives on this page.*

51

organise
verb

administer
command
compere
conduct
control
direct
drive
govern
guide
handle
lead
manage
operate
produce
supervise

outside
noun

boundary
circumference
covering
crust
edge
exterior
perimeter
periphery
profile
shell
silhouette
skin
surface

pain
noun

ache
agony
anguish
backache
cramp
discomfort
distress
earache
headache
hurt
irritation
migraine
spasm
sting
stitch
stomach-ache
suffering
throb
tingling
toothache
torture
twinge

pale
adjective

albino
anaemic
ashy
bleached
blonde
chalky
colourless
creamy
dull
faded
fair
floury
light
milky
pallid
pasty
sallow
subdued
wan
watery
white

plan
verb

arrange
conspire
design
devise
engineer
intend
mastermind
organise
plot
propose
schedule
scheme

play
verb

act
caper
clown
compete
frolic
have fun
jest
romp

pollution
noun

contamination
debris
effluent
filth
garbage
grime
impurity
junk
litter
mess
oil spill
oil slick
refuse
rubbish
sewage
smog
smoke
trash
waste

Hint! *All of these words are things that are bad for the* **environment**. *For more* **environment** *words see page 86.*

poor
adjective

bankrupt
broke
deprived
destitute
disadvantaged
impoverished
meagre
needy
penniless
poverty-stricken
underprivileged
wretched

publication
noun

anthology
atlas
autobiography
bestseller
biography
book
brochure
classic
cookbook
diary
dictionary
directory
edition
encyclopedia
guide
handbook
hardcover
journal
library book
log
magazine
manual
manuscript
memoir
newspaper
notebook
novel
pamphlet
paperback
picture book

pop-up book
recipe book
reference book
school book
series
story book
street directory
textbook
thesaurus
volume
yearbook

push
verb

jerk
jostle
launch
prod
propel
ram
shoulder
shove
thrust

put
verb

deposit
install
lay

load
locate
park
perch
place
rest
set
stack
stick
store
stow

rain
noun

cloudburst
deluge
downpour
drizzle
hail
precipitation
rainfall
rainstorm
shower
sleet
snow
sprinkle
storm
thunderstorm
torrent

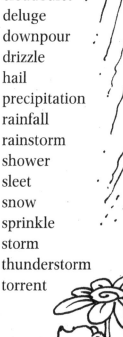

rain
verb

drizzle
hail
pelt
pour
precipitate
shower
sleet
snow
spit
sprinkle
teem

rescue
verb

defend
free
guard
preserve
protect
release
safeguard
salvage
save
secure
shield

rest
noun

break
breather
hibernation
holiday
interruption
leave
leisure time
nap
pause
playtime
relaxation
respite
siesta
sit-down
sleep
snooze
spell
tea-break
time-out
vacation

rest
verb

doze
dream
drowse
hibernate
lay
laze
loaf
nap
pause
relax
remain
retire
sleep
slumber
snooze
wind down

rich
adjective

affluent
aristocratic
classy
fancy
opulent
privileged
prosperous
substantial
wealthy
well-off
well-to-do

ride
verb

balance
canter
cycle
gallop
jog
manoeuvre
pedal
prance
skate
surf
trot

river
noun

aqueduct
brook
canal
channel
creek
spring
stream
tributary
watercourse
waterway

road
noun

alley
avenue
backstreet
boulevard
bypass
causeway
court
crossroads
cul-de-sac
dead end
detour
esplanade

expressway
freeway
grove
highway
lane
motorway
overpass
parade
place
roadway
route
service road
side road
street
terrace
thoroughfare
track
trail

rock
noun

boulder
cobblestone
gravel
rubble
stone

room
noun

apartment
attic
ballroom
basement
bathroom
bedroom
boardroom
cabin
cell
cellar
changing room
chamber
classroom
concert hall
cubicle
darkroom
den
dining room
dormitory
dressing room
kitchen
laundry
lavatory
library
living room
loft
lounge

mess
nursery
office
pantry
playroom
rest room
sauna
staffroom
storeroom
studio
study
suite
surgery
theatre
waiting room
vault

rope
noun

cable
cord
lashing
lasso
lead
line
rein
rigging
skipping

string
tape
thread
tie
tightrope
towrope
tripwire
twine
wire
yarn

rot
verb

corrode
decay
decompose
degenerate
deteriorate
disintegrate
erode
fester
perish
shrivel
stagnate
waste away
wear out
wither

rotten
adjective

bad
decayed
decomposed
degenerated
deteriorated
dilapidated
disintegrated
evil-smelling
filthy
flyblown
foul
perished
polluted
putrid
rancid
rank
spoiled
stinking
tainted
vile
worm-eaten

rough
adjective

bristly
bumpy
chafed
choppy
coarse
harsh
gnarled
grainy
grating
gritty
gravelly
irregular
jagged
jerky
jolty
lumpy
patchy
pebbly
ragged
raw
rickety
rocky
ruffled
rugged
scraggly

shaggy
spiny
tattered
turbulent
uneven
unsettled
whiskery
wrinkled

rule
noun

act
code
command
constitution
convention
custom
decision
formula
instruction
law
maxim
model
motto
order
principle
regulation
ritual
routine
ruling
standard

Hint! *You can form adverbs by adding* **–ly** *or* **–ily** *to many of the adjectives on this page.*

run
verb

bolt
chase
dart
dash
elude
escape
flee
hurry
jog
race
rip
romp
rush
scamper
scoot
scramble
scurry
speed
sprint
stampede
streak

sad
adjective

blue
crestfallen
crushed
dejected
despondent
depressed
discontented
displeased
dissatisfied
distressed
disturbed
doleful
down
forlorn
gloomy
glum
grief-stricken

heartbroken
homesick
hurt
lonely
lonesome
low
melancholic
miserable
moody
mournful
offended
resentful
saddened
sorrowful
sulky
sorry
teary
troubled
unhappy
upset

> **Hint!** *If **running** tires you out why don't you try **walking**? Sprint across to page 73 and have a look.*

sail
verb

circumnavigate
coast
cruise
drift
embark
float
glide
paddle
raft
row
skim
tack
voyage
windsurf

Hint! *Sail across to page 89 for a list of different types of boats.*

save
verb

amass
bank
hoard
hold
invest
keep
put aside
reserve
stack
stockpile
stock up
store
stow

Hint! *To see the verb* **save** *used in another way see* **rescue,** *page 55.*

satisfactory
adjective

adequate
all right
average
common
competent
enough
mediocre
moderate
mundane
okay
ordinary
passable
sufficient
tolerable

Save the whale

say
verb

advise
announce
answer
articulate
ask
babble
blurt
chat
chatter
comment
complain
describe
dictate
exclaim
explain
gasp
gossip
grill
gripe
grumble
inform
interrogate
mention

murmur
mutter
nag
notify
pronounce
purpose
question
quiz
rant
rave
recite
recommend
remark
reply
respond
reveal
scream
shout
snarl
speak
stammer
state
stutter
suggest
talk
tell
utter

vent
vocalise
voice
warn
whine
whisper

scare
verb

alarm
daunt
frighten
haunt
horrify
intimidate
menace
petrify
shock
spook
startle
surprise
terrify
terrorise
threaten

scared
adjective

afraid
agitated
alarmed
apprehensive
distressed
edgy
fearful
frightened
horrific
jittery
jumpy
nervous
nervy
overanxious
panicky
paranoid
petrified
shaky
shocked
spooky
surprised
tense
terrified
timid
traumatised
trembly
uneasy
upset
uptight
worried

search
verb

check
comb
delve
examine
explore
fossick
investigate
probe
pry
ransack
research
rummage
scrutinise
search
seek
snoop
spy on
survey

shout
verb

bawl
bellow
blurt
call
crow
cry
hail

howl
roar
scream
screech
shriek
snap
snarl
wail
yell
yelp

show
verb

appear
demonstrate
disclose
display
emerge
exhibit
expose
flaunt
parade
reveal
surface

Caw

shrink
verb

contact
decrease
deflate
dwindle
fade
reduce
shorten
shrivel
wither

shy
adjective

antisocial
apprehensive
backward
bashful
coy
hesitant
introverted
modest
nervous
quiet
reluctant
reserved
restrained
timid
unassuming
withdrawn

sick
adjective

ailing
anaemic
bedridden
bleary
concussed
dazed
delirious
feeble
feverish
giddy
groggy
ill
indisposed
infirm
injured
malnourished
off-colour
pale
unconscious
unhealthy
unwell
washed out
weak

silly
adjective

absurd
daft
dumb
farcical
foolish
idiotic
ludicrous
mad
nonsensical
preposterous
ridiculous
scatterbrained
senseless
stupid
unintelligent
unwise
zany

Hint! *You can form adverbs by adding –ly or –ily to many of the adjectives on this page.*

slow
adjective

deliberate
dull
idle
inactive
lazy
leisurely
slack
sleepy
sluggish
stagnant
unhurried

smelly
adjective

foul
fragrant
fruity
musky
musty
putrid
rank
savoury
spicy
stinking
stuffy
sweet

smooth
adjective

clean-shaven
even
flat
glassy
horizontal
level
polished
shiny
silky
sleek
slick

soft
adjective

comfortable
cosy
crumbly
delicate
downy
faint
fleecy
flossy
fluffy
furry
fuzzy
inaudible
mashed
muffled

mushy
piano
pianissimo
quiet
silky
sloppy
spongy
squashy
velvety

soil
noun

clay
compost
dirt
earth
ground
loam
minerals
ochre
peat
pebbles
rocks
sand
sediment
subsoil
topsoil

sparkle
verb

beam
blaze
flare
flash
flicker
glare
gleam
glimmer
glint
glisten
glitter
glow
illuminate
shimmer
shine
twinkle

start
verb

begin
commence
depart
establish
initiate
launch
leave
originate
proceed
set out
set up
take off

still
adjective

balanced
calm
firm
fixed
hushed
inactive
inert
motionless
peaceful
quiet
serene
silent
stable
stabilised
stationary
tranquil

stop
verb

abandon
anchor
abort
arrest
barricade
block
brake
beak off
break up
cease
close
conclude
discontinue
end
finish
give up
halt
hinder
hold up
inhibit
intercept
interrupt
intervene
obstruct
oppose
plug
prevent
prohibit
quit
refrain

rest
restrain
retire
shut off
silence
suppress
terminate
withhold

storm
noun

blast
blizzard
cyclone
gale
hail
hurricane
monsoon
rain
rough weather
squall
tempest
thunderstorm
tornado
typhoon
twister
whirlwind
wind

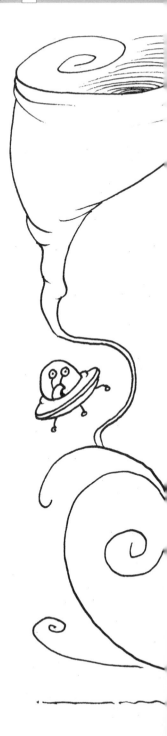

strange
adjective

abnormal
alien
bizarre
crazy
curious
different
eccentric
exotic
extraordinary
foreign
freakish
grotesque
irregular
novel
odd
peculiar
queer
rare
remarkable
uncommon
unconventional
unexplored
unfamiliar
unknown
unrecognised
unsuspected
unusual
weird

strong
adjective

almighty
assertive
athletic
brawny
cyclonic
distinct
domineering
durable
fierce
forceful
hardy
healthy
heavy-duty
hefty
indestructible
influential
insistent
invincible
mighty
muscly
muscular
outspoken
overbearing
potent
powerful
robust
stocky
stout
strong-willed
tough
unstoppable
vigorous
well-built
wiry

Hint! *You can form adverbs by adding –ly or –ily to many of the adjectives on this page.*

sure
adjective

assured
certain
confident
convinced
decided
definite
definitive
guaranteed
positive
self-assured

surprised
adjective

alarmed
amazed
appalled
astonished
astounded
bewildered
flabbergasted
overwhelmed
scared
shocked
spooked
staggered
startled
stunned
taken aback

swim
verb

backstroke
bathe
bob
bodysurf
breaststroke
butterfly
duck-dive
float
glide
paddle
sidestroke
snorkel
surf
tread water
wade

teach
verb

advise
coach
demonstrate
direct
discipline
drill
educate
guide
impart
inform
instruct
introduce
lecture
school
show
train
tutor

tease
verb

aggravate
annoy
antagonise
bother
disturb
harass
hassle
heckle
humiliate
irritate
insult
laugh at
mock
offend
plague
provoke
ridicule
rubbish
taunt
torment
vex

thick
adjective

big
bloated
blubbery
broad
bulky
chunky
clotted
congealed
dense
expansive
extensive
fat
heavy
impenetrable
plump
solid
stocky
stout
stubby
wide

thin
adjective

bony
dainty
delicate
fine
flimsy
gangly
gaunt
lanky
lean
light
little
narrow
petite
puny
scraggy
scrawny
skinny
slender
slight
slim
slinky
small
spindly
wiry
wispy

think
verb

assume
believe
calculate
cogitate
compute
concentrate
conclude
consider
contemplate
deduce
deliberate
devise
estimate
gauge
guess
imagine
judge
measure
meditate
muse
ponder
reason
reckon
reflect
suppose
suspect
wonder

throw
verb

bowl
cast
fling
flip
heave
hurl
hurtle
jerk
launch
pass
pitch
project
send
shoot
skim
sling
thrust
toss
whirl

tidy
adjective

arranged
coordinated
methodical
neat
orderly
organised
trim
well-groomed

tired
adjective

exhausted
fatigued
footsore
lethargic
run-down
sleepy
weary
worn-out

top
noun

apex
brink
cap
ceiling
climax
crest
crown
culmination
head
high point
hilltop
peak
pinnacle
roof
summit
tip
vertex
zenith

Hint! *If you slip off the **top** you end up at the **bottom**. See page 10 for the opposite of **top**.*

town
noun

capital
central business
  district
city
community
country town
fishing town
ghost town
hamlet
home town
metropolis
mining town
municipality
seaport
settlement
suburb
township
village

trip
noun

daytrip
drive
excursion
expedition
fall
hike
jaunt
journey
joy-ride
outing
patrol
pilgrimage
safari
saunter
spin
stroll
tour
trek
vacation
voyage
walk
wander

true
adjective

accurate
actual
authentic
certain
constant
correct
earnest
exact
factual
faithful
frank
genuine
honest
loyal
proper
real
reliable
right
sincere
steady
straight
trustworthy
truthful
valid

try
verb

aim
attempt
endeavour
experiment
sample
strive
tackle
taste
test
undertake

ugly
adjective

awful
beastly
crude
disgusting
distorted
dreadful
foul
frightful
ghastly

grim
gross
grotesque
gruesome
hideous
horrible
horrid
messy
monstrous
nasty-looking
offensive
plain
rank
repulsive
revolting
terrible
unattractive
unpleasant
unsightly
vile

unfair
adjective

biased
chauvinistic
discriminatory
dishonest
hypercritical
ill-treated
improper
inequitable
narrow-minded
one-sided
partial
persecuted
prejudiced
undeserved
unjust
unjustified
unsportsmanlike
wrong

walk
verb

accompany
amble
creep
cross
escort
follow
hobble
limp
lumber
march
pace
pad
parade
promenade
plod
pound
saunter
scramble
shuffle
slog
sneak
stagger
step
stride
stroll
strut
stumble
swagger
toddle
totter
tramp
trudge
waddle

want
verb

crave
desire
fancy
hope
long
need
require
wish
yearn

wave
noun

beach comber
breaker
ripple
shore break
surf
surge
swell
tidal wave
tsunami
tube
whitecap

weak
adjective

debilitated
delicate
deficient
exhausted
defenceless
diluted
faint
feeble
flimsy
frail
fragile
helpless
inadequate
incapable
incapacitated
ineffective
infirm
insipid
invalid
lame
pathetic
powerless
sickly
slight
unprotected
unconvincing
unsatisfactory

wet
adjective

boggy
clammy
damp
dank
drenched
drizzly
flooded
humid
immersed
marshy
moist
muddy
rainy
showery
sloppy

soaked
sodden
soggy
sopping
submerged
submersed
sticky
swamped
sweaty
torrential
waterlogged

wet
verb

bathe
dampen
dip

drench
douse
duck
flood
hose
immerse
irrigate
moisten
moisturise
saturate
shower
soak
splash
splatter
spray
sprinkle
squirt
swamp
water

wild
adjective

aggressive
barbaric
berserk
bloodthirsty
brutal
cruel
distraught
ferocious
fierce
forceful
frantic
frenzied
furious
intense
mad
passionate
potent
powerful
profound
reckless
rough
rugged
savage
severe
strong
stormy
turbulent
unbroken
uncivilised
uncontrollable
uncultivated
unmanageable
untrained
violent
vivid
volcanic
wayward

Hint! *If these* ***wild*** *words are too ferocious for you, then check out the entry for* ***calm*** *on page 13.* ***Calm*** *is the opposite of* ***wild***.

wind
noun

air current
airflow
blast
blizzard
blow
breeze
cross-wind
current
cyclone
draught
dust storm
gale
gust
headwind
hurricane
monsoon
puff
sea breeze
squall
storm
tail wind
tornado
turbulence
twister
typhoon
whirlwind
willy-willy
zephyr

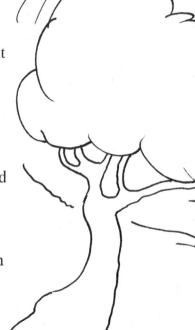

woman
noun

adult
aunt
beauty
dame
daughter
duchess
female
girlfriend
granddaughter
grandmother
granny
lady
lass
madam
miss
mother
mum
niece
person
princess
queen
sister
wife
witch

work
verb

act
achieve
function
labour
make
manage
operate
perform
produce
slave
study
toil

worry
verb

bother
concern
disturb
fret
irritate
panic
pester

plague
torment
trouble
vex

wreck
verb

botch
bungle
contaminate
corrupt
damage
demolish
destroy
devastate
mutilate
pollute
ruin
sabotage
shatter
spoil
tear down
vandalise
wipe out

wrong
adjective

abnormal
absurd
bad
crazy
evil
exaggerated
false
faulty
harmful
illegal
illogical
immoral
improper
inaccurate

inappropriate
inconsistent
incorrect
irrational
irrelevant
mistaken
misunderstood
naughty
offensive
outrageous
prejudiced
unacceptable
unjustified
unnatural
unsuitable
untrue
villainous
wicked

Hint! *You can form adverbs by adding* **–ly** *or* **–ily** *to many of the adjectives on this page.*

young
adjective

adolescent
babyish
boyish
childish
fresh
girlish
immature
inexperienced
infant
junior
juvenile
minor
new
pubescent
teenage
toddler
undeveloped
youthful

APPENDIXES – *Useful wordlists*

ANIMALS

 birds

albatross
bellbird
butcherbird
budgerigar
canary
chicken
cockatoo
crow
dodo (extinct)
dove
duck
eagle
emu
finch
fowl
galah
goose
gull
hawk
hen
honeyeater
kiwi
kookaburra
lyrebird
magpie
mutton-bird
ostrich
owl
parrot
pelican
penguin
pigeon
plover
quail
robin
rooster
rosella
seagull
sparrow
swan
turkey
wedge-tailed eagle
willie wagtail

 cats

Abyssinian
Burmese
cheetah
cougar
feline
jaguar
Manx
leopard
lion
lynx
mountain lion
ocelot
panther
Persian
puma
puss
Siamese
snow leopard
tabby
tiger
wildcat

 **dogs**

Afghan
Alsatian
basset hound
beagle
bloodhound
blue heeler
border collie
boxer
bulldog
bull-terrier
cattle dog
chihuahua
cocker spaniel
corgi
dachshund
Dalmatian
dingo
Doberman
fox terrier
German shepherd
golden retriever
Great Dane
greyhound

husky
Irish setter
Jack Russell
kelpie
labrador
mongrel
Old English
 sheepdog
Pekingese
pointer
poodle
pug
red setter
Rhodesian
 ridgeback
Rottweiler
sheepdog
spaniel
terrier
watchdog
whippet
wolfhound

domestic animals

bird
bull
cat
cow
donkey
goat
goldfish
guinea pig

horse
mouse
pig
pony
rabbit
sheep
tortoise
turtle

fish

carp
catfish
cod
cuttlefish
eel
goldfish
marlin
mullet
parrotfish
piranha
salmon
shark
snapper
stingray
stonefish
swordfish
trout
tuna
whiting

insects

ant
bee
beetle
blowfly
borer
bug
bull ant
butterfly
cicada
cockroach
cricket
dragonfly
earwig
flea
fly
fruit fly
glow-worm
gnat
grasshopper
grub
hornet
ladybird
larva
leech
locust
louse
mantis
mosquito
moth
nit
sandfly
silverfish
soldier ant

stick insect
termite
tick
wasp

lizards

blue-tongue
chameleon
frill-necked lizard
goanna
gecko
iguana
komodo dragon
legless lizard
skink
tuatara
water dragon

sea creatures

abalone
barnacle
clam
cowry
crab
crayfish
dolphin
jellyfish
lobster
mussel
octopus

oyster
periwinkle
porpoise
prawn
scallop
sea anemone
seahorse
seal
sea lion
sea snail
stingray
walrus

sharks

bronze whaler
bull shark
grey nurse
gummy shark
hammerhead
mako
tiger shark
thresher shark
whale shark
white pointer
wobbegong

snakes

adder
anaconda
asp
black snake
boa constrictor
brown snake
carpet snake
cobra
copperhead
death adder
diamond python
grass snake
king cobra
mamba
python
rattlesnake
red-bellied black
  snake
sea snake
serpent
taipan
tiger snake
viper
water snake

spiders

bird-eating spider
black widow
daddy-long-legs
funnel-web
garden spider
huntsman
katipo
money spider
orb spider
red-back
Saint Andrew's
  Cross spider
tarantula
trapdoor spider
white-tailed spider
wolf spider

 ## whales

baleen whale
beluga whale
blue whale
humpback
killer whale
narwhal
orca
pilot whale
right whale
sperm whale
white whale

 ## wild animals

alligator
anteater
antelope
ape
baboon
badger
bandicoot
bat
bear
buffalo
camel
chimpanzee
crocodile
deer
dingo
echidna
elephant
fox
frog
gazelle
giraffe
goanna
gorilla
hippopotamus
hyena

jaguar
kangaroo
leopard
lion
lizard
llama
monkey
moose
orangutan
panda
panther
polar bear
possum
puma
raccoon
reindeer
rhinoceros
snake
tiger
toad
turtle
wallaby
wild boar
wolf
wombat
yak
zebra

animal babies

cat – kitten
cow – calf
deer – fawn
dog – puppy
duck – duckling
elephant – calf
frog – tadpole
goat – kid
goose – gosling
horse – colt (male)
     – filly (female)
     – foal (either)
insect – larva
lion – cub
kangaroo – joey
pig – piglet
seal – pup
sheep – lamb
swan – cygnet
tiger – cub

animal groups

ants – colony/nest
bees – swarm
birds – flock
cattle – herd
cows – herd
crows – murder
dogs – pack
elephants – herd
fish – shoal/school
geese – gaggle
hens – brood
horses – herd
insects – swarm
kangaroos – mob
kittens – litter
rabbits – nest
seals – pod
sheep – flock/mob
snakes – nest
whales – pod/herd
wolves – pack

Australian and New Zealand native animals

bandicoot
dingo
echidna
emu
kakapo
kangaroo
kiwi
koala
kookaburra
numbat
platypus
possum
saltwater crocodile
Tasmanian devil
tuatara
wallaby
weka
wombat

BUILDINGS

apartment
barracks
cabin
castle
chalet
church
college
construction
convent
cottage
council chambers
dwelling
farmhouse
flats
hall
hangar
high-rise
home
homestead
hospital
hostel
hotel
house
hut
inn
library
manor
mansion
mess
monastery
motel
office
palace

place
ranch
residence
school
shack
shed
shop
shopping centre
skyscraper
stable
stadium
station
structure
tower
unit
town hall
villa

CIVICS

bureaucracy
citizen
citizenship
city
community
constitution
council
councillor
government
mayor
municipality
nation
ombudsman
people
politician
politics
premier
prime minister
rights

COLOURS

black

charcoal
coal
ebony
grey
jet black
pitch black
raven

blue

aqua
cerulean
cobalt
indigo
ocean blue
peacock blue
navy
sapphire
sky blue
turquoise

brown

almond
auburn
beige
bronze
caramel
chestnut
cocoa
coffee
copper
chocolate
fawn
ginger
hazel
khaki
tan
terracotta

green

avocado
bottle green
forest green
emerald
grass green
jade
lime
olive
sea green
teal

orange

apricot
peach
rust
saffron
sienna
tangerine

purple

aubergine
fuchsia
lavender
lilac
mauve
plum
royal purple

red

blood red
brick red
burgundy
cerise
coral
crimson
deep pink
fire red
garnet
maroon
rose
ruby
salmon
scarlet
vermilion

white

chalk
cream
ivory
pearl
vanilla

yellow

buttercup yellow
canary yellow
champagne
gold
lemon
mustard
sand
wheat

COMPUTERS

backup
byte
cursor
database
desktop
disk
email
hardware
icon
internet
keyboard
laptop
menu
modem
mouse
network
password
printer
processor
program
screen
software
terminal
tool bar
website
World Wide Web

DINOSAURS

allosaurus
ankylosaurus
brachiosaurus
brontosaurus
diplodocus
diprotodon
giant wombat
iguanodon
mammoth
mastodon
plesiosaurus
pterodactyl
stegosaurus
triceratops
tyrannosaurus

ENVIRONMENT

air
conservation
earth
ecology
ecosystem
evolution
habitat
landcare
life
nature
plants
pollution
recycling
renewable
resource
soil
water

FRUIT

apple
apricot
avocado
banana
berry
blackberry
blueberry
cherry
currant
date
fig
grape
grapefruit
guava
kiwi fruit
lemon
lychee
mandarin
mango
melon
nectarine
olive
orange
papaya
passionfruit
pawpaw
peach
pear
pineapple
plum
prune
raisin
raspberry
redcurrant
rockmelon
strawberry
sultana
tomato
watermelon

RELATIVES

ancestor
aunt
brother
child
cousin
family
father
foster-child
foster-parent
grandchild
grandfather
grandmother
grandparents
great-aunt
great-uncle
kin
mother
nephew
next of kin
niece
parent
sister
stepchild
stepfather
stepmother
uncle

SCIENCE

atom
apparatus
bacteria
biology
chemical reaction
chemistry
electron
equipment
experiment
gas
geology
hypothesis
laboratory
liquid
magnifying glass
measurement
microscope
neutron
Petri dish
physics
procedure
proton
scientist
solid

SHOPS

bakery
barber
beauty salon
bookshop
butcher
chemist
corner store
delicatessen
department store
dry-cleaner
fashion shop
fish and chip shop
florist
greengrocer
grocer
hairdresser
hardware store
market
milk bar
newsagency
pawnshop
pet shop
pharmacy
second-hand store
sports store
stall
supermarket
toy shop
video store

SPACE

asteroid
astronaut
astronomer
astronomy
black hole
comet
constellation
cosmos
Earth
galaxy
Jupiter
Mars
Mercury
meteor
Milky Way
moon
Neptune
observatory
orbit
planet
satellite
Saturn
solar system
spacecraft
star
sun
telescope
Uranus
Venus

TRANSPORT

 aircraft

aeroplane
airbus
airliner
biplane
bomber
charter plane
Concorde
crop duster
fighter
glider
hang-glider
Harrier
helicopter
Hercules
hot air balloon
hydroplane
interceptor
jet
jumbo
seaplane
space shuttle
Spitfire
Tiger moth
triplane

boats

aircraft carrier
barge
battleship
cabin cruiser
canoe
cargo ship
catamaran
cruiser
destroyer
dinghy
ferry
fishing trawler
gondola
houseboat
hulk
hydrofoil
icebreaker
junk
kayak
launch
lifeboat
motorboat
ocean liner
oil tanker
paddle-steamer
punt
raft
rowing boat
sailing boat
ship
ski-boat
speedboat
steamboat
troop carrier
tugboat
vessel
yacht

 motor vehicles

automobile
beach buggy
bobcat
bus
campervan
coach
convertible
coupé
dirt bike
dragster
dump truck
four-wheel drive
hatchback
hot rod
jalopy
jeep
limousine
lorry
mini-bus
mobile home
motorcycle
off-road vehicle
panel van
prime mover
quad bike
racing car
recreational
  vehicle
sedan
semitrailer
sports car
station wagon
tank
taxi
tractor
troop-carrier
truck
van

 trains

diesel train
express train
freight train
goods train
locomotive
special
steam train

VEGETABLES

asparagus
beans
bean sprouts
bok choy
broccoli
brussels sprouts
cabbage
capsicum
carrot

cauliflower
celery
corn
cucumber
eggplant
leek
lentils
lettuce
maize
mushroom
onion

parsley
parsnip
peas
potato
pumpkin
silverbeet
soybeans
spinach
sprouts
turnip
zucchini

INDEX